# One Pot

## Everyday recipes to enjoy

Bath • New York • Singapore • Hong Kong • Cologne • Delhi
Melbourne • Amsterdam • Johannesburg • Shenzhen

# spiced chicken stew

## ingredients

**SERVES 6**

1.8 kg/4 lb chicken pieces

2 tbsp paprika

2 tbsp olive oil

25 g/1 oz butter

450 g/1 lb onions, chopped

2 yellow peppers, deseeded
    and chopped

400 g/14 oz canned chopped
    tomatoes

225 ml/8 fl oz dry white wine

450 ml/16 fl oz chicken stock

1 tbsp Worcestershire sauce

$1/2$ tsp Tabasco sauce

1 tbsp finely chopped fresh
    parsley, plus extra
    to garnish

325 g/11$1/2$ oz canned
    sweetcorn kernels, drained

425 g/15 oz canned butter
    beans, drained and rinsed

2 tbsp plain flour

4 tbsp water

salt

## method

**1** Season the chicken pieces well with salt and dust with the paprika.

**2** Heat the oil and butter in a flameproof casserole or large saucepan. Add the chicken pieces and cook over a medium heat, turning, for 10–15 minutes, or until browned all over. Transfer to a plate with a slotted spoon.

**3** Add the onions and peppers to the casserole. Cook over a low heat, stirring occasionally, for 5 minutes, or until softened. Add the tomatoes, wine, stock, Worcestershire sauce, Tabasco sauce and parsley and bring to the boil, stirring. Return the chicken to the casserole, cover and simmer, stirring occasionally, for 30 minutes.

**4** Add the sweetcorn and butter beans to the casserole, partially re-cover and simmer for a further 30 minutes, or until the chicken is tender and the juices run clear when a skewer is inserted into the thickest part of the meat. Place the flour and water in a small bowl and mix to make a paste. Stir a ladleful of the cooking liquid into the paste, then stir the paste into the stew. Cook, stirring frequently, for a further 5 minutes. Garnish with parsley and serve immediately.

# red hot chilli chicken

## ingredients

**SERVES 4**

1 tbsp curry paste

2 fresh green chillies, chopped

5 dried red chillies

2 tbsp tomato purée

2 garlic cloves, chopped

1 tsp chilli powder

pinch of sugar

pinch of salt

2 tbsp groundnut or
   sunflower oil

$^1/_2$ tsp cumin seeds

1 onion, chopped

2 curry leaves

1 tsp ground cumin

1 tsp ground coriander

$^1/_2$ tsp ground turmeric

400 g/14 oz canned chopped
   tomatoes

150 ml/5 fl oz chicken stock

4 skinless, boneless chicken
   breasts

1 tsp garam masala

fresh mint sprigs,
   to garnish

cooked rice, to serve

## method

**1** To make the chilli paste, place the curry paste, fresh and dried chillies, tomato purée, garlic, chilli powder, sugar and salt in a blender or food processor. Process into a smooth paste.

**2** Heat the oil in a large, heavy-based saucepan. Add the cumin seeds and cook over a medium heat, stirring constantly, for 2 minutes, or until they begin to pop and release their aroma. Add the onion and curry leaves and cook, stirring, for 5 minutes.

**3** Add the chilli paste and cook for 2 minutes, then stir in the ground cumin, coriander and turmeric and cook for a further 2 minutes.

**4** Add the tomatoes and stock. Bring to the boil, then reduce the heat and simmer for 5 minutes. Add the chicken and garam masala, cover and simmer gently for 20 minutes, or until the chicken is tender and the juices run clear when a skewer is inserted into the thickest part of the meat. Garnish with mint sprigs and serve immediately with rice.

# italian turkey

## ingredients

SERVES 4

1 tbsp olive oil

4 turkey escalopes or steaks

2 red peppers, deseeded
    and sliced

1 red onion, sliced

2 garlic cloves, finely chopped

300 ml/10 fl oz passata

150 ml/5 fl oz medium white
    wine

1 tbsp chopped fresh
    marjoram

400 g/14 oz canned cannellini
    beans, drained and rinsed

3 tbsp fresh breadcrumbs

salt and pepper

fresh basil sprigs, to garnish

## method

**1** Heat the oil in a flameproof casserole or heavy-based frying pan. Add the turkey escalopes and cook, turning occasionally, over a medium heat for 5–10 minutes, or until golden. Transfer to a plate.

**2** Add the peppers and onion to the casserole and cook over a low heat, stirring occasionally, for 5 minutes, or until softened. Add the garlic and cook for a further 2 minutes.

**3** Return the turkey to the casserole and add the passata, wine and marjoram. Season to taste with salt and pepper. Bring to the boil, then reduce the heat, cover and simmer, stirring occasionally, for 25–30 minutes, or until the turkey is tender and the juices run clear when a skewer is inserted into the thickest part of the meat.

**4** Preheat the grill to medium. Stir the cannellini beans into the casserole and simmer for a further 5 minutes. Sprinkle the breadcrumbs over the top and place under the preheated grill for 2–3 minutes, or until golden. Garnish with basil sprigs and serve immediately.

# beef & baby onion casserole

## ingredients

**SERVES 6**

2 tbsp olive oil

450 g/1 lb baby onions, peeled but kept whole

2 garlic cloves, halved

900 g/2 lb stewing steak, cubed

$1/2$ tsp ground cinnamon

1 tsp ground cloves

1 tsp ground cumin

2 tbsp tomato purée

700 ml/$1^1/4$ pints red wine

grated rind and juice of 1 orange

1 bay leaf

salt and pepper

chopped fresh flat-leaf parsley, to garnish

mashed potatoes, to serve

## method

**1** Preheat the oven to 150°C/300°F/Gas Mark 2. Heat the oil in a large flameproof casserole and cook the whole onions and garlic, stirring frequently, for 5 minutes, or until soft and beginning to brown. Add the beef and cook over a high heat, stirring frequently, for 5 minutes, or until browned all over.

**2** Stir the spices and tomato purée into the casserole and season to taste with salt and pepper. Pour in the wine, scraping any sediment from the base of the casserole, then add the orange rind and juice and the bay leaf. Bring to the boil and cover.

**3** Cook in the preheated oven for 2 hours. Remove the lid from the casserole and return to the oven for a further hour, stirring once or twice, until the beef is tender. Remove and discard the bay leaf and garnish with parsley and serve immediately with mashed potatoes.

# chilli con carne

## ingredients

**SERVES 4**

750 g/1 lb 10 oz lean
   stewing steak

2 tbsp vegetable oil

1 large onion, sliced

2–4 garlic cloves, crushed

1 tbsp plain flour

425 ml/15 fl oz tomato juice

400 g/14 oz canned chopped
   tomatoes

1–2 tbsp sweet chilli sauce

1 tsp ground cumin

425 g/15 oz canned red
   kidney beans, drained and
   rinsed

1/2 tsp dried oregano

1–2 tbsp chopped fresh
   parsley, plus extra
   to garnish

salt and pepper

tortilla chips, to serve

## method

**1** Preheat the oven to 160°C/325°F/Gas Mark 3. Using a sharp knife, cut the beef into 2-cm/ ¾-inch cubes. Heat the oil in a large flameproof casserole. Add the beef in batches and cook over a medium heat, stirring, until browned all over. Remove the beef from the casserole with a slotted spoon and reserve.

**2** Add the onion and garlic to the casserole and fry until lightly browned, then stir in the flour and cook for 1–2 minutes.

**3** Stir in the tomato juice and tomatoes and bring to the boil. Return the beef to the casserole and add the sweet chilli sauce, cumin and salt and pepper to taste. Cover and cook in the preheated oven for 1½ hours, or until the beef is almost tender.

**4** Remove the casserole from the oven and stir in the kidney beans, oregano and parsley. Taste and adjust the seasoning, adding salt and pepper if needed. Cover the casserole and return to the oven for 45 minutes. Garnish with parsley and serve immediately with tortilla chips.

# sausage & bean casserole

## ingredients

**SERVES 4**

8 Italian sausages

3 tbsp olive oil

1 large onion, chopped

2 garlic cloves, chopped

1 green pepper, deseeded
    and sliced

400 g/14 oz canned chopped
    tomatoes

2 tbsp sun-dried tomato paste

400 g/14 oz canned cannellini
    beans, drained and rinsed

## method

**1** Prick the sausages all over with a fork. Heat 2 tablespoons of the oil in a large flameproof casserole. Add the sausages and cook over a low heat, turning frequently, for 10–15 minutes, until evenly browned and cooked through. Remove them from the casserole and keep warm. Drain off the oil and wipe out the casserole with kitchen paper.

**2** Heat the remaining oil in the casserole. Add the onion, garlic and green pepper and cook, stirring occasionally, for 5 minutes, or until softened.

**3** Add the tomatoes and leave the mixture to simmer for about 5 minutes, stirring occasionally, or until slightly reduced and thickened.

**4** Stir the sun-dried tomato paste, cannellini beans and sausages into the mixture. Cook for 4–5 minutes, or until piping hot. Add a little water if the mixture becomes too dry during cooking. Serve immediately.

# chorizo, chilli & chickpea casserole

## ingredients

**SERVES 4**

2 tbsp olive oil

1 onion, sliced

1 large yellow pepper,
    deseeded and sliced

1 garlic clove, crushed

1 tsp chilli flakes

225 g/8 oz chorizo sausage

400 g/14 oz canned chopped
    tomatoes

400 g/14 oz canned
    chickpeas, drained

handful of rocket leaves

salt and pepper

roughly chopped fresh basil,
    to garnish

cooked rice, to serve

## method

**1** Heat the oil in a flameproof casserole and fry the onion over a medium heat, stirring occasionally, for 5 minutes. Add the yellow pepper, garlic and chilli flakes and cook for 2 minutes, stirring.

**2** Chop the chorizo into bite-sized chunks and stir into the casserole. Add the tomatoes and chickpeas with salt and pepper to taste. Bring to the boil, cover and simmer for 10 minutes.

**3** Stir the rocket into the casserole. Garnish with basil and serve immediately with rice.

# lamb & potato moussaka

## ingredients

**SERVES 4**

1 tbsp olive oil

1 onion, finely chopped

1 garlic clove, crushed

350 g/12 oz fresh lean lamb
    mince

250 g/9 oz mushrooms, sliced

425 g/15 oz canned chopped
    tomatoes with herbs

150 ml/5 fl oz lamb stock

2 tbsp cornflour

2 tbsp water

1 large aubergine, sliced

500 g/1 lb 2 oz potatoes,
    parboiled for 10 minutes
    and sliced

2 eggs

125 g/4$^{1}/_{2}$ oz soft cheese

150 ml/5 fl oz natural yogurt

55 g/2 oz mature Cheddar
    cheese, grated

salt and pepper

## method

**1** Preheat the oven to 190°C/375°F/Gas Mark 5. Heat the oil in a large saucepan. Add the onion and garlic and cook for 3–4 minutes. Add the lamb and mushrooms and cook, stirring frequently over a medium heat for 5 minutes, or until browned all over. Stir in the tomatoes and stock, bring to the boil and simmer for 10 minutes.

**2** Mix together the cornflour and water to make a smooth paste, then stir into the saucepan. Cook, stirring constantly, until thickened.

**3** Spoon half the lamb mixture into an ovenproof dish. Cover with the aubergine slices, then top with the remaining lamb mixture. Arrange the potato slices on top.

**4** Beat together the eggs, soft cheese and yogurt. Season to taste with salt and pepper, then pour over the potatoes to cover. Sprinkle over the Cheddar cheese and bake in the preheated oven for 45 minutes, or until the topping is set and golden brown. Serve immediately.

# catalan fish stew

## ingredients

**SERVES 4–6**

large pinch of saffron threads

4 tbsp almost-boiling water

6 tbsp olive oil

1 large onion, chopped

2 garlic cloves, finely chopped

1$\frac{1}{2}$ tbsp chopped fresh thyme

2 bay leaves

2 red peppers, deseeded and
    roughly chopped

800 g/1 lb 12 oz canned
    chopped tomatoes

1 tsp smoked paprika

250 ml/9 fl oz fish stock

140 g/5 oz blanched almonds,
    toasted and finely ground

12–16 live mussels, scrubbed
    and debearded

12–16 live clams, scrubbed

600 g/1 lb 5 oz skinless,
    boneless hake or cod
    fillets cut into 5-cm/2-inch
    chunks

12–16 raw prawns, peeled and
    deveined

salt and pepper

## method

**1** Put the saffron threads in a heatproof jug with the water and leave to infuse for at least 10 minutes.

**2** Heat the oil in a large flameproof casserole over a medium–high heat. Reduce the heat to low and cook the onion, stirring occasionally, for 10 minutes, or until golden but not browned. Add the garlic, thyme, bay leaves and peppers and cook, stirring frequently, for 5 minutes, or until the peppers and onions have softened.

**3** Add the tomatoes and paprika and simmer, stirring frequently, for a further 5 minutes.

**4** Stir in the stock, the saffron and its soaking liquid and the almonds and bring to the boil, stirring. Reduce the heat and simmer for 5–10 minutes, until the sauce reduces and thickens. Season to taste with salt and pepper.

**5** Meanwhile, discard any mussels or clams with broken shells and any that refuse to close when tapped.

**6** Gently stir the hake into the stew so that it doesn't break up, then add the prawns, mussels and clams. Reduce the heat to very low, cover and simmer for 5 minutes, or until the hake is opaque, the mussels and clams have opened and the prawns have turned pink. Discard any mussels or clams that remain closed. Serve immediately.

# salmon & herbs in prosciutto parcels

## ingredients

**SERVES 4**

2 bunches of mixed fresh
  herbs, such as coriander,
  parsley, basil and dill
125–175 ml/4–6 fl oz extra
  virgin olive oil
4 salmon fillets, about
  200 g/7 oz each
8 slices of prosciutto
salt

## method

**1** Preheat the oven to 180°C/350°F/Gas
Mark 4. Roughly chop the mixed herbs and put in
a mortar, season with a little salt and pound with
a pestle. Gradually work in the oil to make a
thick paste.

**2** Spread the herb paste evenly over the tops of
the salmon fillets, then wrap each fillet in two
slices of prosciutto.

**3** Place on a large baking sheet and bake in the
preheated oven for 20–25 minutes. Transfer to
warmed serving plates and serve immediately.

# clams in black bean sauce

## ingredients

**SERVES 4**

900 g/2 lb live clams,
　　scrubbed

1 tbsp vegetable or groundnut
　　oil

1 tsp finely chopped fresh
　　ginger

1 tsp finely chopped garlic

1 tbsp rinsed and chopped
　　fermented black beans

2 tsp Chinese rice wine

1 tbsp finely chopped spring
　　onion

1 tsp salt

## method

**1** Discard any clams with broken shells and any that refuse to close when tapped.

**2** Preheat a wok with a lid, then add the oil. Stir-fry the ginger and garlic until fragrant. Add the black beans and cook for 1 minute.

**3** Over a high heat, add the clams and rice wine and stir-fry for 2 minutes to mix everything together. Cover and cook for about 3 minutes. Remove and discard any clams that remain closed. Add the spring onion and salt. Serve immediately.

# ribollita

## ingredients

**SERVES 4**

3 tbsp olive oil

2 red onions, roughly chopped

3 carrots, sliced

3 celery sticks, roughly
   chopped

3 garlic cloves, chopped

1 tbsp chopped fresh thyme

400 g/14 oz canned cannellini
   beans, drained and rinsed

400 g/14 oz canned chopped
   tomatoes

about 600 ml/1 pint water or
   vegetable stock

2 tbsp chopped fresh parsley

500 g/1 lb 2 oz cavolo nero or
   Savoy cabbage, cored and
   sliced

1 small day-old ciabatta loaf,
   torn into small pieces

salt and pepper

extra virgin olive oil,
   to serve

## method

**1** Heat the olive oil in a large saucepan and cook the onions, carrots and celery, stirring frequently, for 10–15 minutes. Add the garlic, thyme, and salt and pepper to taste. Continue to cook for a further 1–2 minutes, until the vegetables are golden.

**2** Add the cannellini beans to the pan and pour in the tomatoes. Add enough of the water to cover the vegetables.

**3** Bring to the boil, then reduce the heat and simmer for 20 minutes. Add the parsley and cavolo nero and cook for a further 5 minutes.

**4** Stir in the bread and add a little more water, if needed. The consistency should be thick.

**5** Taste and adjust the seasoning, adding salt and pepper if needed. Ladle into warmed bowls and serve immediately, drizzled with extra virgin olive oil.

# spring vegetable frittata

## ingredients

**SERVES 2**

15 g/$^1$/$_2$ oz pine kernels

5 eggs

55 g/2 oz fine asparagus
    spears

55 g/2 oz French beans

55 g/2 oz fresh shelled baby
    broad beans or peas

1 tsp olive oil

10 g/$^1$/$_4$ oz butter

25 g/1 oz fresh Parmesan
    cheese shavings

handful of rocket leaves

salt and pepper

crusty bread, to serve

## method

**1** Toast the pine kernels in a 20-cm/8-inch heavy-based frying pan with a heatproof handle over a medium heat, stirring until they are golden brown. Tip out onto a plate. Using a fork, lightly beat the eggs in a bowl with salt and pepper to taste.

**2** Preheat the grill to high. Half-fill the frying pan with water and bring to the boil. Add the asparagus, French beans and broad beans. Simmer for 2 minutes, then drain.

**3** Dry the pan and return to a medium heat. Add the oil and butter and, when melted and foaming, add the vegetables and pour the beaten eggs over the top. Cook the frittata for 1–2 minutes, until lightly browned underneath, then place the pan under the preheated grill and cook for 1–2 minutes, until just set in the middle.

**4** Pile the Parmesan cheese shavings and rocket on top of the frittata and scatter with the pine kernels. Serve immediately with crusty bread.

# cauliflower bake

## ingredients

**SERVES 4**

500 g/1 lb 2 oz cauliflower, broken into florets and parboiled

600 g/1 lb 5 oz potatoes, cut into small cubes and parboiled

100 g/3$^1$/$_2$ oz cherry tomatoes

### cheese sauce

25 g/1 oz butter or margarine

1 leek, sliced

1 garlic clove, crushed

3 tbsp plain flour

300 ml/10 fl oz milk

85 g/3 oz mixed cheese, such as Cheddar, Parmesan and Gruyère cheese, grated

$^1$/$_2$ tsp paprika

2 tbsp chopped fresh flat-leaf parsley

salt and pepper

## method

**1** Preheat the oven to 180°C/350°F/Gas Mark 4. To make the cheese sauce, melt the butter in a large saucepan. Add the leek and garlic and cook over a low heat for 1 minute. Stir in the flour and cook, stirring, for 1 minute. Remove from the heat, then gradually stir in the milk, 55 g/2 oz of the cheese, the paprika and parsley. Return to the heat and bring to the boil, stirring. Season to taste with salt and pepper.

**2** Transfer the cauliflower and potatoes to a deep ovenproof dish and top with the cherry tomatoes. Pour the cheese sauce over to cover and sprinkle with the remaining cheese.

**3** Cook in the preheated oven for 20 minutes, or until the vegetables are cooked through and the cheese is golden brown and bubbling. Serve immediately.

# mediterranean vegetables with feta & olives

## ingredients

**SERVES 4**

1 red onion, sliced into thick
    rings

1 small aubergine, thickly
    sliced

2 large mushrooms, halved

3 red peppers, halved and
    deseeded

3 plum tomatoes, peeled and
    diced

2 garlic cloves, very finely
    chopped

1 tbsp chopped fresh
    flat-leaf parsley

1 tsp chopped fresh rosemary

1 tsp dried thyme or oregano

finely grated rind of
    1 lemon

75 g/2³/₄ oz stale, coarse
    breadcrumbs

3 tbsp olive oil, plus extra for
    brushing

6–8 black olives, stoned and
    sliced

25 g/1 oz feta cheese (drained
    weight), cut into 1-cm/
    ¹/₂-inch cubes

salt and pepper

## method

**1** Preheat the grill. Put the onion, aubergine, mushrooms and peppers on a large baking tray, placing the peppers cut-side down. Brush with a little oil. Cook under the preheated grill for 10–12 minutes, turning the onion, aubergine and mushrooms halfway through, until beginning to blacken. Cut into even-sized chunks.

**2** Preheat the oven to 220°C/425°F/Gas Mark 7. Place the grilled vegetables in a shallow ovenproof dish. Arrange the tomatoes on top. Season to taste with salt and pepper.

**3** In a bowl, combine the garlic, parsley, rosemary, thyme and lemon rind with the breadcrumbs. Season to taste with pepper. Add the oil to bind the mixture together. Scatter the breadcrumb mixture over the vegetables, followed by the olives and feta cheese.

**4** Bake in the preheated oven for 10–15 minutes, or until the vegetables are heated through and the topping is crisp. Serve immediately.

This edition published by Parragon Books Ltd in 2013

Parragon Books Ltd
Chartist House
15–17 Trim Street
Bath BA1 1HA, UK
www.parragon.com

ISBN: 978-1-4723-2692-8

Printed in China

**Notes for the Reader**
This book uses both metric and imperial measurements. Follow the same units of measurement throughout; do not mix metric and imperial. All spoon measurements are level: teaspoons are assumed to be 5 ml, and tablespoons are assumed to be 15 ml. Unless otherwise stated, milk is assumed to be full fat, eggs and individual vegetables are medium, and pepper is freshly ground black pepper. Unless otherwise stated, all root vegetables should be washed in plain water and peeled prior to using.

Garnishes, decorations and serving suggestions are all optional and not necessarily included in the recipe ingredients or method.

The times given are an approximate guide only. Preparation times differ according to the techniques used by different people and the cooking times may also vary from those given. Optional ingredients, variations or serving suggestions have not been included in the time calculations.

Recipes using raw or very lightly cooked eggs should be avoided by infants, the elderly, pregnant women, convalescents and anyone suffering from an illness. Pregnant and breastfeeding women are advised to avoid eating peanuts and peanut products. Sufferers from nut allergies should be aware that some of the ready-made ingredients used in the recipes in this book may contain nuts. Always check the packaging before use.